CAPE BRETON

TASTES

CAPE BRETON
TASTES

Recipes from Cape Breton's Best Restaurants
with Gary Walsh

Photographs by
Warren Gordon

NIMBUS
PUBLISHING

Nimbus Publishing Limited
PO Box 9166
Halifax, NS   B3K 5M8
(902) 455-4286
www.nimbus.ca

Printed and bound in China

Design: Kate Westphal, Graphic Detail Inc., Charlottetown, PE
Gary Walsh photo: Carol Kennedy
Warren Gordon photo: Katheryn Gordon
Photo on page 17 courtesy of Premium Seafoods

Library and Archives Canada Cataloguing in Publication

Walsh, Gary, 1950-

Cape Breton tastes : recipes from Cape Breton's best restaurants /
Gary Walsh ; photographs by Warren Gordon.

ISBN 13: 978-1-55109-657-5   ISBN 10: 1-55109-657-9

1. Cookery—Nova Scotia—Cape Breton Island. 2. Restaurants—Nova
Scotia—Cape Breton Island. I. Gordon, Warren, 1951- II. Title.

TX715.6.W345 2008   641.59716'9   C2007-907150-3

The Canada Council | Le Conseil des Arts
for the Arts | du Canada

NOVA SCOTIA
Tourism, Culture and Heritage

We acknowledge the financial support of the Government of Canada through
the Book Publishing Industry Development Program (BPIDP) and the Canada
Council, and of the Province of Nova Scotia through the Department of
Tourism, Culture and Heritage for our publishing activities.

table of contents

introduction

On Cape Breton Island, the land reaches up to the sky and is caressed by the sea. Turn in any direction and you will be inspired by a seascape or a landscape or a chance meeting with a resident happy to give you a smile and a wave. These qualities of great beauty and human warmth are also the ingredients of wonderful cooking. It is impossible to be in Cape Breton without experiencing food—from church suppers to crab and lobster dinners, mussel festivals, strawberry and blueberry festivals, and a potpourri of other cultural celebrations and festivals. On a Saturday in July, one can have breakfast at the Farmers' Market in Sydney, lunch at a strawberry festival in Millville, and supper at an all-you-can-eat crab dinner in Indian Brook.

One of my favourite food experiences on a sunny day in Cape Breton is to spend the morning driving to bakeries and fruit stands in search of good tea biscuits and fresh strawberries, then whipping some cream, sitting on my deck, and eating strawberry shortcake. And if the strawberries have passed, the blueberries are on their way. At my house, a breakfast of blueberry pancakes is another favourite.

The chefs and restaurants of Cape Breton will guide you through a delicious journey in this book—and Cape Breton is a journey. World-famous scenery and a relaxed pace of living are everywhere. There are many places to stop and look, many trails to walk, and much music for listening and dancing. And there is always food. So take a deep breath and relax. Visit one of these restaurants and take some time to savour the fresh and succulent fare, and always expect a conversation and a friendly smile. Don't be surprised if someone calls you "hon" or asks you who your father is—it's just part of the trip.

The food presented here is a sample of what's available on Cape Breton Island. Whether you are looking for a bowl of chowder and a homemade biscuit or an evening meal watching the sunset in Inverness, this is the right place. The recipes in this book can be enjoyed both at home or in the restaurant. Either way, the tastes of Cape Breton are sure to bring you comfort and pleasure.

Enjoy the scenery, the music, the people, and the food of Cape Breton. There's a lot to go around.

facing page: Neils Harbour

tempting tastes

Everyone knows about the Cabot Trail and the many exciting views and attractions it offers. But Cape Breton Island has an abundance of small communities and rich cultural regions, each of which reflects the diversity of eating experiences. Acadian food in Cheticamp and Isle Madame reaches back into the island's history and tantalizes taste buds. Seafood chowder is a staple of many restaurants, and arguments abound over the best version. New culinary experiences mix with tradition to make every dish a tempting taste.

facing page: Margaree

chicken fricot with bannock

Makes 6–8 portions.

Bannock

4 cups flour
4 teaspoons baking powder
1/2 teaspoon salt
1/2 cup vegetable oil
1 3/4 cup water

Combine all ingredients together in a large bowl. Mix well. Add flour to clean surface for kneading dough. Knead mixture ten to twelve times on floured surface. Do not over-knead, as dough may be sticky. Form large ball and place in a large baking dish or a cast iron frying pan. Bake at 425°F for 30–35 minutes. Baste top of loaf with butter when out of the oven. Serve with butter and molasses.

Fricot

3–4 pound utility chicken
1 large onion, diced in large pieces
4 tablespoons butter
1 tablespoon flour
1 1/2 teaspoons salt
1/2 teaspoon summer savory
3 cups carrots, cut large
3 cups potatoes, cut large
Pepper, dash

Boil chicken with salt, pepper, and enough water to cover chicken on medium heat in a large pot. Remove chicken from stock and remove bones and skin (chicken is done when bones separate easily from meat). Set chicken aside and let cool. Sauté onions in butter until soft. Bring stock to a boil and add onions and carrots. Boil vegetables in stock for 10 minutes, add potatoes and boil for another 10 minutes. Add chicken pieces and summer savory to pot and simmer slowly until vegetables are firm but cooked. Let cool for 10 minutes, then thicken slightly with flour and about 1/2 cup water. Serve with cranberry sauce on the side.

L'Auberge Acadienne
Arichat

Ingonish Bay, Smokey Mountain

chicken tikka soup

Makes 8–10 bowls.

Chicken marinade

2–3 pounds boneless, skinless
  chicken breasts
8 ounces plain yogurt (10% m.f.)
4 teaspoons garlic, minced
4 teaspoons fresh ginger, minced
2–3 teaspoons red chili, minced
2 teaspoons paprika
1 teaspoon turmeric
1 teaspoon cardamom
1 teaspoon ground cumin
1 teaspoon ground pepper
1 teaspoon salt
1/2 teaspoon ground mace

Cut chicken into strips. Blend marinade ingredients in a food processor and mix thoroughly with chicken strips. Marinate at least 4 hours, or overnight.

Remove chicken from marinade and grill on each side until cooked. Set aside excess marinade for the soup.

Soup base

1/4 pound butter
1 pound onions, chopped
2–3 teaspoons red chili, minced (or to taste)
2 teaspoons fresh ginger, chopped
1 teaspoon garlic
1 teaspoon garam masala
6 cups chicken or vegetable stock
2/3 cup flour
1 pound cooked yellow split peas
8 ounces plain yogurt (plus extra for drizzling)
2 cups cream (10% m.f.)
1 small bunch cilantro, chopped
Salt, to taste

Melt butter in a soup pot. Add onions, chili, ginger, garlic, and garam masala. Cover, and cook slowly for 5 minutes. Stir in the flour and cook for 2–3 minutes. Add excess marinade and peas. Heat stock in a separate pan, then add to vegetables. Bring to a boil and simmer for about 10 minutes. Purée in a food processor (in batches if necessary) until almost smooth.

Pour puréed soup into large bowl or container. Stir in yogurt, cream, and most of cilantro. Ladle into bowls, gently float chicken on top, and sprinkle with cilantro. Place a couple of dollops of yogurt on top and serve. Garnish with remaining cilantro.

Water's Edge
Baddeck

Baddeck

multigrain bread

Makes 4 loaves.

3 1/2 cups whole wheat flour
4 1/2 cups unbleached white flour
1/4 cup gluten flour
7/8 cup rolled oats
1/2 cup soy grits
1/4 cup millet
3 teaspoons salt
1/2 cup sunflower seeds
1/4 cup sesame seeds
1/4 cup honey (or malt)
1/4 cup canola oil
1 cup buttermilk
3 1/3 cups warm water
5 teaspoons instant yeast

In a large bowl, combine whole wheat flour, white flour, gluten flour, oats, soy grits, millet, salt, sunflower seeds, and sesame seeds. Make a well in the centre, and add oil and honey. Whisk yeast into warm water and buttermilk in a separate dish.

Combine buttermilk mixture with flour mixture. Mix together and turn out onto floured counter. Knead for 10–12 minutes then return back to bowl, cover, and allow to rise for 1 1/2 hours in a warm place.

Once dough has risen, uncover, punch down, and cover for another 45 minutes. Turn dough onto floured counter, divide into four equal pieces, shape into loaves, and place in greased loaf pans. Allow to rise for another 1–1 1/2 hours.

Preheat oven to 350°F. Bake for 45–55 minutes. Cool on wire rack.

The Herring Choker Café
Nyanza

Nyanza

curried lentil soup

Makes 4–6 bowls.

3/4 cup red lentils
1 large red onion
3 teaspoons olive oil (or butter)
4 cups water
1 1/2–2 teaspoons honey
4 teaspoons curry powder
2 teaspoons sea salt
2 teaspoons turmeric
1/4–1/2 teaspoon cayenne
1/4–1/2 teaspoon ground cumin
1/4–1/2 teaspoon coriander
Cinnamon, to taste
Ground cloves, to taste

Sauté onions in oil for 5 minutes. Add lentils and water. Bring to a boil, then reduce temperature to medium high and simmer for about 15 minutes. Add remaining ingredients and let simmer for another 5 or 10 minutes.

Open Café
North Sydney

Sydney Harbour

pâté à la viande (meat pie)

Makes 4 pies.

Filling

3 pounds boneless stewing pork
1 1/2 pounds boneless stewing beef
1 tablespoon salt
1/2 tablespoon pepper
1/2 tablespoon onion salt
1 tablespoon chives
1/2 pound onions, chopped

Mix all ingredients together in a pot and add water to cover meat. Bring to a boil. Simmer about three hours, or until tender. Once cooled, shred meat into very thin strips by hand (meat should come apart easily).

Pastry

3 cups flour
1 teaspoon salt
3 teaspoons baking powder
1/3 pound pure lard
1 egg
1 cup skim milk

Mix flour, salt, baking powder, and pure lard in a large bowl. Add milk gradually and mix with a fork until all flour is absorbed. For each pie, roll two crusts. Place first crust in bottom of pie pan, fill with meat mixture, and cover with second crust. Beat egg gently and brush on top of second crust. Bake at 450°F until crust is golden.

Restaurant Acadien
Cheticamp

Presqu'ile

Neils Harbour

fabulous fish

The mention of seafood is enough to brighten the eyes of chefs in Cape Breton. Wonderful flavours create opportunities for new dishes built on the foundations of tried-and-true recipes. It all begins with lobster and salmon, but the bounty of the sea is rich and varied. The fishing industry remains a central element of life on Cape Breton Island, stretching back to the Mi'kmaq. Cape Bretoners anxiously await the first day of lobster or crab season, but rest assured, we'll save enough to go around.

seafood chowder

Makes 20 bowls.

2 pounds mussels
2 cups water
2 cups white wine
1 cup celery, finely chopped
1 1/2 cups onion, finely chopped
3 tablespoons garlic, finely chopped
1/2 pound bacon, finely chopped
6 cups potato, diced
2 1/2 pounds haddock
2 1/2 pounds halibut
1 pound salmon
1 pound scallops
1 pound shrimp
4 cups cream (18%)
2 teaspoons dill
Dash white pepper
Salt, to taste

Sauté onion, celery, garlic, and bacon in a heavy-bottom pot until tender, and set aside. Add water and wine to a second pot with a steamer insert. Add mussels and steam until opened. Remove mussels from pot. Add haddock and halibut to pot and steam until done (about 2–3 minutes). Remove haddock and halibut and set aside. Add shrimp and scallops to steamer pot. Steam until barely done (about 1–2 minutes). Boil potato in separate pot and cool. Combine all ingredients in a large pot. Add cream, dill, pepper, and remaining liquid from steamer pot. Add salt to taste.

Cranberry Cove Inn
Louisbourg

Mabou Beach

smoked salmon quiche

Makes 8 portions.

Crust

1 1/2 cups all-purpose flour
1/4 teaspoon salt
1/2 cup butter, chilled
1 large egg
1/4 teaspoon vinegar
2 tablespoons cold water

With two knives or a pastry blender, cut the butter into flour and salt. Add egg, vinegar, and water. Mix and work softly into a ball. Flatten dough and press it into a metal loose-bottom, 9-inch tart pan so that dough is up to the fluted rim of the pan. Prick bottom and sides of dough with a fork and cover dough with plastic wrap. Let cool in the refrigerator for 1 hour or overnight.

Preheat the oven to 350°F. Remove the plastic wrap and line the dough with foil. Fill the pan with dry beans and bake dough for 20 minutes. This blind baking will ensure crust keeps its shape.

Filling

8 ounces smoked salmon, chopped
1 small onion, diced
4 eggs
1/4 teaspoon sugar
1 cup whipped cream (35% m.f.)
1/2 teaspoon fresh dill
1/4 teaspoon coarse pepper

Whisk eggs, sugar, dill, and coarse pepper. Add whipped cream.

Take the pan from the oven and remove the beans and the foil. Arrange smoked salmon bits and diced onion in the crust and pour in filling mixture. Bake at 350°F for 15 minutes. Reduce heat to 325°F and bake for 20–25 minutes until quiche is firm. Cool at least 10 minutes before serving.

Cape Breton Smokehouse
Malagawatch

acadian shrimp

Makes 5 servings.

Shrimp Marinade

2 teaspoons Cajun spices
1/2 fresh lemon, squeezed
1 1/2 teaspoons Worcestershire sauce
Tabasco sauce
30 fresh or frozen large peeled shrimp
   (21–25 count)

Sauce

3 teaspoons shallots, finely chopped
2 cloves garlic
2 teaspoons parsley
2 teaspoons butter
2 teaspoons olive oil
1 tablespoon brandy
1/2 cup white wine
1/4 cup (35% m.f) cream
Salt
Pepper

In a mixing bowl, combine four marinade ingredients and shrimp. Let mixture set in the fridge for about 10 minutes.

For sauce, heat olive oil over medium-high heat in a frying pan. Add marinated shrimp and sauté for a few seconds. Pour brandy into pan and flambé the shrimp mixture until brandy evaporates. Add shallots, garlic, and butter, and sauté for 1 to 2 minutes. Add white wine and cream. Let simmer for 2 minutes. Remove shrimp, put aside, and reduce temperature or remaining liquid. Simmer for 3 to 4 minutes. Add salt and pepper to taste. Transfer shrimp back into the sauce and bring to a boil. Serve over rice pilaf or pasta, and garnish with parsley.

Bras d'Or Lakes Inn
St. Peter's

Big Baddeck

shrimp and scallop flambé

Makes 2 servings.

12 large scallops (20–30 count), washed
12 large shrimp (20–26 count), washed and de-veined
2 tablespoons garlic butter
2 ounces brandy
8 tablespoons hollandaise sauce
8 tablespoons béchamel sauce
2 ounces Pernod

Melt garlic butter in a flambé pan. Add scallops, and cook 1 minute per side. Add shrimp and cook for 1 minute per side. Remove scallops and shrimp from heat and drain off excess liquid. Return empty pan back to high heat to get the pan hot for flambé. Pour brandy into the pan. When pan is flaming, stir in hollandaise and béchamel sauce. Add Pernod and stir sauce in with the shrimp and scallops. Serve with choice of potato and vegetable.

Grubstake Restaurant
Louisbourg

Lighthouse Point, Louisbourg

Pleasant Bay

lakeside seafood cannelloni

Makes 8 servings.

Filling

32 pieces (1–2 boxes) oven-ready cannelloni
14 ounces (1 jar) tomato sauce
1425 grams (3 x 475g) ricotta cheese
1 cup Parmesan cheese, shredded
1 red pepper, diced
1 yellow pepper, diced
6 cloves garlic, minced
2 cups fresh spinach, shredded
2 tablespoons olive oil
Salt and pepper to taste

Heat olive oil in large pan. Add garlic and sauté lightly. Add peppers and cook until just soft. Add salt and pepper and spinach, cover, and steam for 2 minutes. Remove mixture from pan, straining excess liquid. Place in refrigerator.

Combine ricotta and Parmesan in a large bowl. Add cooled pepper mixture. Combine well. Set aside in fridge for 1 hour.

With a piping bag, stuff each piece of cannelloni with filling. Place in baking pan and cover with tomato sauce. Bake in preheated 350°F oven until soft, about 20–30 minutes.

Topping

14 ounces (1 jar) tomato sauce
16 large shrimp
16 large scallops
1 pound mussels
5 cloves garlic, minced
1/2 cup white wine
Parmesan cheese
Fresh chives, chopped

In a pot, heat up tomato sauce.

In a frying pan, sear shrimp and scallops on each side, 8 at a time. Add them to tomato sauce to finish cooking.

In the same frying pan, sauté garlic. Add mussels and white wine. Cover and steam 2–3 minutes. Add to tomato sauce.

To serve, place 4 pieces of cannelloni on a plate. Cover with 2 shrimp, 2 scallops, 6–8 mussels and some tomato sauce. Top with grated Parmesan and sprinkle with chopped fresh chives.

Inverary Inn
Baddeck

Inverary Inn

seafood explosion

Makes 2 servings.

10 tiger shrimp
10 Digby scallops
4–6 ounces fresh-shelled lobster meat
12 mussels
2 tablespoons garlic butter
1/2 cup whipping cream
6–8 teaspoons green pepper, diced
4 teaspoons mushrooms, finely chopped
2–4 teaspoons pesto
Parmesan cheese
1 cup pasta (fettuccine or linguine)

Sauté mushrooms and green peppers in garlic butter. Stir in pesto. Add whipping cream, shrimp, scallops, lobster meat, and mussels. Sauté in a pan for 2–3 minutes, then reduce heat. Add cooked pasta and mix thoroughly, allowing flavours to permeate pasta. Top with fresh Parmesan.

The Lobster Galley
South Haven

Seal Island lighthouse

poached halibut with leek-velouté sauce

Makes 4 servings.

Leek-velouté sauce

For this sauce it is very important that you make your own fish stock. The stock can be prepared in advance and kept frozen. Do not use fish bouillon. Try to get some codfish heads or fish bones from haddock or halibut.

Codfish heads or fish bones (from white fish only)
1 leek, chopped
2 onions, chopped
2 carrots, chopped
2–3 celery sticks, chopped
1 cup white wine
2 leeks, rinsed and finely chopped
1 cup whipping cream
Salt, to taste
White pepper, to taste
Paprika, to taste

Combine fish with onions, carrots, celery, 1 leek and a little paprika, salt, and white pepper. Add enough water to cover ingredients and bring to a boil. Simmer for one to three hours on low heat. Strain through cheesecloth. Add white wine and reduce to one third. Set aside 1 cup of this fish stock for poaching halibut. Cook 2 finely chopped leeks for twenty minutes in the reduced sauce. Purée with a stick blender and strain again. Add whipping cream and boil until liquid is creamy, but not too thick. Add salt and pepper to taste.

Halibut

4 fillets fresh halibut
4 slices smoked salmon
8 fresh oysters, shucked, in shells
4 grape leaves
2 cups white wine (chardonnay or pinot gris)
4 slices lemon
Sprigs of fresh dill to garnish
1 tablespoon butter
1 cup fish stock
A bouquet garni: a mix of fresh basil, thyme, dill, and oregano (for poaching liquid)

Use a deep skillet with a lid. Pour in fish stock, place four grape leaves in the bottom, and place one halibut fillet on top of each grape leaf. Add herbs, cover with the lid, and let liquid come to a quick boil, then immediately turn off the heat. Let fish sit covered for five minutes.

Carefully lift fish fillets, still on the grape leaves, from the skillet and arrange on a serving plate. Place a rolled up slice of smoked salmon on top of fish, and garnish with fresh dill. Arrange two oysters around each piece of fish. Serve with couscous and steamed vegetables, as well as velouté sauce on the side (don't pour sauce over fish). Garnish with lemon slices.

Chef Lars Willum
Cape Breton Gourmet

Joan Harris Cruise Pavilion,
Big Ceilidh Fiddle

salmon amandine and dauphinois

Serves 4.

White dill sauce

1 1/4 cups milk
1/4 onion, chopped
1 bay leaf
2 cloves
2 tablespoons unsalted butter
2 tablespoons flour
3 tablespoons fresh dill, chopped
Salt and pepper, to taste

Combine milk, onion, bay leaf, chopped dill, and cloves in a pot and simmer for 15 minutes. Remove from heat, discard solid, and keep liquid. In another pot, melt butter. Add flour and stir until flour and butter are combined. Remove from heat and cool slightly. Combine both pots into one and whisk on medium heat to eliminate any lumps.

20–24 ounces salmon (four good-sized pieces)
4 tablespoons roasted almonds
12 tablespoons white dill sauce
8 tablespoons red and yellow pepper, finely chopped
4 sprigs dill

Place salmon on hot grill. Grill all sides (about 2 minutes each side). When ready to serve, place salmon on plate, then pour dill sauce and sprinkle almonds over salmon. Garnish with chopped red and yellow pepper and sprigs of dill.

Dauphinois

2 large potatoes, peeled and thinly sliced
1 onion, peeled and thinly sliced
1/2 cup Parmesan cheese
2 cups heavy cream
1/2 cup cheddar cheese
Dash of salt and pepper

Preheat the oven to 325°F. Butter an 8 x 8-inch pan. Place a layer of potatoes, then a layer of onions, and then a layer of 1/8 cup of Parmesan cheese over the top. Keep making these three layers until ingredients are used. Pour heavy cream on top, sprinkle with cheddar cheese, and add salt and pepper to taste. Cover with foil and cook for approximately 20–25 minutes in preheated oven. Remove from oven, let sit for 5–7 minutes, and cut into triangles. Serve with salmon.

Normaway Inn
Margaree

Margaree

bouillabaisse

Makes 4 servings.

Broth

8 cups fish stock
8 cups chicken stock
1 cup white wine
1/4 cup olive oil
1 large celery branch, diced
1 medium carrot, diced
2 medium onions, diced
2 cloves garlic, thinly sliced
1 teaspoon fennel seeds
1 teaspoon coriander seeds
5 black peppercorns
1 small stick cinnamon
1 bay leaf
Generous pinch of saffron threads
3 orange slices (peel on)

Fish ingredients

30–35 mussels (washed and beard cleaned)
12 large (21–25 count) shrimp
  (peeled, de-veined, and with tail on)
12 scallops (20–30 count), cut into
  large chunks
8–12 ounces halibut (or other white fish),
  cut into large chunks
8–12 ounces salmon, cut into large chunks

In a heavy-bottom pot, add oil and sweat garlic and onions slowly until translucent but do not brown. Add fennel seeds, coriander seeds, peppercorns, bay leaf, cinnamon, and saffron until aromatic and saffron colour blooms. Deglaze with white wine and allow to reduce slightly. Add celery, carrots, orange slices, chicken stock, and fish stock. Bring to a boil and reduce to a simmer. Reduce broth by half. Adjust seasoning to taste.

With stock on a gentle simmer, add mussels. When mussels have opened, add in order: salmon, then shrimp, then halibut, then scallops. Pause briefly (10–15 seconds) between each subsequent addition. Discard any mussels which did not open during cooking and serve in wide shallow bowls. Accompany with crusty bread.

The Markland Coastal Resort
Dingwall

Neils Harbour

memorable meals

One of the great pleasures of Cape Breton Island is the pace of life. Surrounded by so many natural wonders, it is easy to relax and savour dinner. As the evening fades and the sun sets, memories are formed, friendships deepened, and romances rekindled.

More and more of our restaurants are offering fine Nova Scotia wines—some from grapes grown on our island. Try one and be sure to ask about Johnny Grape. Cape Breton wines, Cape Breton scenery, and inventive Cape Breton chefs will make all your evenings worth telling your friends about.

polenta florentine with three cheeses

Makes 6 servings.

5 cups water
1 1/2 cups coarse-ground polenta
1/2 teaspoon salt
4 ounces mozzarella cheese
4 ounces provolone cheese
12 ounces frozen spinach (or fresh equivalent)
1/3 cup asiago cheese, grated
2 cups marinara sauce, heated
2 tablespoons fresh oregano, chopped
2 tablespoons fresh parsley, chopped

In a medium saucepan over medium heat, bring water to a boil. Gradually add polenta and salt, stirring constantly. Cook, stirring often, for 30 minutes or until polenta thickens and is creamy. Wilt spinach (place washed leaves in a pan and bake at high heat).

Add mozzarella and provolone, stirring until cheese is melted and well-blended. Evenly divide polenta among 6 shallow bowls. Top polenta with spinach and marinara, and sprinkle with oregano, parsley, and asiago.

Chanterelle Inn
North River

North River

classic greek roast leg of lamb with lemon-garlic potatoes

Serves 6–8.

1 eight-pound leg of lamb (bone in)
2 tablespoons olive oil
6 pounds roasting potatoes
1 cup olive oil
1 cup lemon juice
4 garlic cloves, peeled and slivered
1–2 tablespoons oregano
1/4 cup water
Salt
Pepper

Dry Rub

4 garlic cloves, peeled and slivered
2 tablespoons oregano
2 tablespoons thyme
2 tablespoons rosemary
1 teaspoon whole black peppercorns
Salt

Trim lamb of excess fat. Make 10–15 incisions with a sharp paring knife. Stuff the incisions with the rub, using any remainder to rub the surface of the lamb. Season to taste with salt and pepper. Rub with olive oil.

Preheat oven to 375°F. Cut potatoes lengthwise into about six wedges per potato, and place in a roasting pan. Add olive oil, lemon juice, garlic, oregano, water, salt, and pepper to the potatoes.

Place lamb on potatoes. Bake for 1 hour and 45 minutes until well done, basting frequently. Remove from oven. Let lamb cool for ten minutes before carving. Keep potatoes warm until ready to serve.

Fourna Grill
Sydney

Sydney Harbour

beef ragout

Makes 6–8 portions.

2–3 pounds stewing beef, cubed
1 piece lard, cubed
12 carrots, sliced (pieces about 1-inch thick)
1 large turnip, cubed
6 onions, sliced
1 1/2 cups flour
1 cup red wine vinegar
1 green pepper
Bay leaves
Fresh thyme and tarragon (oregano is an
**   acceptable substitute)**
Fresh Italian (flat leaf) parsley

Toss beef in enough vinegar to coat the pieces. Cut green pepper and bay leaves into large pieces to release their flavour and add to beef. Cover beef and let marinate in cool place for an hour.

Remove beef from marinade and discard bay leaves. Coat beef and lard chunks with flour and place in a large, oven-safe casserole dish. Put this preparation into a 450°F oven.

Remove the dish after about 30 minutes or when beef has begun to brown and render a bit of gravy. Add onions, carrots, and turnips, fresh herbs (thyme, tarragon, and parsley) with stems, and mix well. Add water to half the height of the contents and mix well. Cover the dish with foil and bake at 350°F. Remove after one hour and mix well. Taste the sauce and season if necessary. If sauce is still thin, mix one cup of flour with two ladles of liquid from marinade dish and add to main casserole dish. Bake for another 1 1/2 hours. Remove from oven and serve.

Hôtel de la Marine
Fortress of Louisbourg

Fortress Louisbourg
overleaf: St. Mary's Church, East Bay

pork geschnetzeltes with spätzle

Makes 3–4 servings.

Pork geschnetzeltes

3 pounds pork loin
10 mushrooms, sliced
1/4 cup white wine
2 cups cream
Salt and pepper to taste
Butter
1 tablespoon flour

Slice pork loin into very thin strips. Place in pan and fry in butter until no pink is visible. Add mushrooms. Sprinkle flour in pan with pork and mushrooms. Add wine and mix well. Whisk cream into mixture and simmer until thick. If sauce becomes too thick, thin with milk.

Spätzle

2 eggs
1 teaspoon salt
3/4 cup water
1/4 cup milk
2 cups flour
1 tablespoon salt

Beat together eggs, 1 teaspoon salt, water, and milk in a large bowl. Slowly whisk flour into wet ingredients to make a dough. Bring large pot of water, with one tablespoon of salt, to a boil. Place dough mixture on a cutting board and slice small pieces into boiling water. Boil for five minutes, stirring once. Drain and rinse with cold water. Fry pieces in butter until golden brown.

Riverbank Restaurant
Marion Bridge

Two Rivers Wildlife Park, Myra River

vegetarian moussaka

Makes 6–8 servings.

2 medium eggplants
3 cups mushrooms, chopped in quarters
2 roasted sweet red peppers
2 medium zucchini, sliced diagonally
1 cup fine bread crumbs
4 cups tomato sauce (good quality)
1/4 cup fresh basil, chopped
3 teaspoons salt

For the béchamel sauce:

1/4 cup flour
1/4 cup butter
2 cups milk
1/2 teaspoon nutmeg
1 teaspoon fresh ground pepper
Pinch of salt
1 cup fresh Parmesan cheese, grated

Melt butter until it foams. Add flour and cook for 3 minutes, stirring constantly with a whisk. Add milk, stirring constantly until thickened. Add nutmeg, pinch of salt, and pepper. Remove from heat and add grated Parmesan.

Slice eggplant into 1/2-inch slices. Sprinkle with 3 teaspoons salt and let sit for 30 minutes to remove bitter juices. Pat dry with paper towel and bake on oiled baking sheet at 350°F for 30 minutes.

Oil an 8 x 10-inch pan and line with half of the eggplant, half sliced zucchini, and roasted peppers. Combine mushrooms, tomato sauce, basil, and bread crumbs in a bowl. Add mixture to pan and top with remainder of zucchini and eggplant. Top with béchamel sauce and sprinkle with bread crumbs and parmesan. Bake at 350°F for one hour.

Bankhead Pub
Inverness

Inverness Beach

smokey mountain strip loin with dauphine potatoes and roasted garlic herb jus

Makes 8 servings.

Dauphine potatoes

1/2 cup butter
1 cup water
2 tablespoons salt
1 cup all-purpose flour, sifted
4 large eggs
2 1/2 pounds (7–8 medium) potatoes
1 tablespoon ground nutmeg
1/8 tablespoon black pepper
1 cup Asiago cheese, grated
1 1/2 cup crispy smoked bacon, chopped

Bring butter, water, and salt to a boil in a 1-quart saucepan. Add flour all at once. Stir over low heat until mixture leaves side of pan and forms ball (1–2 min). Cool slightly.

Beat in one egg at a time until a sticky paste results (Chou paste). Peel potatoes, boil and mash until fluffy. Add to Chou paste. Add in Asiago cheese and smoked bacon. Shape into log-shaped pieces (1-inch in diameter) and fry in fat at 375°F for 2–3 minutes or until lightly browned. Drain on paper towel.

8 (ten-ounce) Smokey Mountain (New York cut) beef strip loins

Marinade

4 tablespoons fresh oregano, chopped
2 tablespoons garlic, chopped
1 tablespoon black peppercorns, crushed
4 tablespoons canola oil

Mix together and brush over strip loins. Grill strip loin as desired.

Roasted garlic herb jus

1/2 cup garlic cloves, peeled
1 tablespoon canola oil
1/2 cup white wine
1/4 cup water
Salt and pepper
2 cups beef jus

In a medium fry pan, sauté garlic in canola oil on medium heat for 1 minute until lightly browned. Deglaze the pan with white wine and reduce the liquid until it disappears and the garlic begins to caramelize in its own oils. Season with salt and pepper. Deglaze again with water and reduce until water disappears and garlic is golden brown and soft. Cool slightly and mash with a fork. Add mashed garlic to beef jus and bring to a boil. Serve over and around strip loin.

Keltic Lodge
Ingonish

apple and brie stuffed chicken breast

Makes 6 servings.

6 (seven-ounce) boneless skinless chicken breasts
12 slices Granny Smith apple (about 1/4 inch thick)
12 slices Brie cheese (little thicker than apple)
12 slices prosciutto ham
12 tablespoons butter

Pan-fry apple slices in butter until golden brown and let cool. Form a pocket in chicken breast by slicing along the side and open it up. Slide two apple and two Brie slices into the pocket of chicken. Use two prosciutto slices to wrap around chicken breast, making sure to cover the pocket. Pan-fry with breast side down until golden brown, then turn over and finish in 375°F oven for about 10 minutes.

Sauce

1 medium shallot, minced
1/2 cup trio chardonnay
2 cups heavy cream
1 tablespoon unsalted butter
1 1/2 tablespoons lemon juice
Salt and pepper, to taste

Add shallots and chardonnay to a saucepan, reduce by three-quarters, then add heavy cream and reduce by half, or until desired consistency is achieved. Stir in unsalted butter and lemon juice, and add salt and pepper to taste.

Island Sunset Resort
Belle Cote

Margaree Harbour

roast goose with dried fruit and cranberry stuffing

Makes 8 servings.

Stuffing (begin 4 hours ahead)

1 (twelve-ounce) package of mixed dried
   fruit (prunes, apricots, apples, etc.)
1 medium onion, minced
16 ounces fresh cranberries
1 cup sugar
5 cups day-old bread cubes, lightly packed
1 teaspoon salt
1/2 teaspoon ground allspice
2 1/4 cups water

In a saucepan over high heat, heat 2 cups water, fruit, and onions to boiling. Reduce heat to low. Simmer 15 minutes or until fruit is tender. Pour mixture into a large bowl. In the same pan over medium heat, heat 1/4 cup water, cranberries, and sugar to boiling. Reduce heat to low and simmer for 7 minutes or until berries pop, stirring occasionally. Drain liquid from berries and pour berries into fruit mixture. Add bread cubes, salt, and allspice. Toss lightly.

1 (ten-pound) goose (allow 1–1 1/2 pounds
   goose per serving)

If frozen, ensure goose is properly defrosted. Remove the neck and giblets from goose. Discard fat from body cavity, rinse and drain. Stuff goose lightly with cranberry stuffing. Skewer neck skin to back. Tie legs and tail together. Place goose breast side up on a wire rack in an open roasting pan. Prick the skin all over with a two-tined fork. Roast at 350°F for 3 1/2 hours or until thermometer in goose reads 190°F. When goose is done, remove to a platter. Remove string from around legs and tail.

Sherry gravy

1 (thirteen-ounce) can chicken broth
3 tablespoons all-purpose flour
1/4 cup cold water
3 tablespoons sherry

Remove fat from drippings in the pan, leaving juice and brown bits. Add sherry and light mixture on fire. Wait for flames to die out. Stir in broth. Over a medium heat, bring to a boil. Blend flour and water in a cup and gradually stir this into the hot mixture and cook, stirring continuously, until thickened, approximately 10 minutes. Serve with goose and stuffing.

English Country Garden Bed and Breakfast
Indian Brook

Gaelic College of Celtic Arts and Crafts

sensational sweets

A cup of tea or coffee and a good dessert are essential to Cape Breton cuisine. Baking is a mainstay of our kitchens. Everyone has a special tea biscuit or oatcake recipe usually passed down from a grandmother or aunt. Squares and cookies are always in the pantry. Fresh fruit and chocolate abound.

We even manage to use our famous Glen Breton Whisky to create an unforgettable cake. By the way, if you try these recipes at home, remember—never make boiled icing on a humid day.

chocolate cake with boiled icing

Makes 1 cake.

Cake

1 cup cocoa
1 cup water
1 cup milk
1/2 cup butter
2 cups white sugar
2 teaspoons vanilla
2 eggs
2 cups flour
2 teaspoons baking soda
1/2 teaspoon salt

Icing

2 cups brown sugar
2 egg whites
6 teaspoons cold water
Pinch of salt

In a saucepan, combine cocoa, water, and milk. Whisk until smooth and bring to a boil. Remove from heat and add butter, stirring to melt. Stir in white sugar and vanilla. In a separate bowl, beat eggs slightly and whisk into chocolate mixture. In a separate bowl, combine flour, baking soda, and salt. Stir into chocolate mixture and whisk until smooth.

Pour batter mixture into two 8-inch round pans. Bake at 350°F for 30 minutes, or until top springs back when lightly touched.

Combine all icing ingredients in a double boiler. Beat on high until icing forms fluffy but firm peaks. Spread on cooled cake.

Cedar House Bakery and Restaurant Boularderie

Seal Island bridge

custard apple cream pie

Makes 1 pie.

1 pastry for 9-inch pie shell
  (your own or a mix)
1 cup granulated sugar
6 tablespoons all-purpose flour
4 tablespoons cornstarch
2 pounds medium cooking apples, peeled,
  cored, and cut into wedges
2 eggs
2 cups sour cream
1/4 cup sugar
1/2 teaspoon ground cinnamon

Maple sauce

3 cups brown sugar
1/2 cup water
1 tablespoon butter
1/2 teaspoon maple syrup

Roll out pastry and line 9-inch glass pie plate. Flute edge if desired. Combine 1 cup granulated sugar, flour, and cornstarch in large bowl. Add apples and stir until coated. Turn into pie shell. Spread evenly. Mix eggs and sour cream in a small bowl. Spread evenly over apple mixture. Combine 1/4 cup sugar and cinnamon in a small dish. Sprinkle over sour cream mixture. Bake on bottom rack in a 350°F oven for about 75 minutes until crust is golden and apples are tender but crisp. Cool to room temperature before cutting. Cut into 8 wedges.

Combine all sauce ingredients in a saucepan. Bring to a boil, reduce heat to simmer and cook for 10–15 minutes. Pour over pie wedges and serve.

Dundee Resort
Dundee

Dundee

Aspy Bay

fresh fruit pavlova

Makes 12 meringues.

Fresh fruit and berries (cantaloupe, honeydew melon, pineapple, green grapes, strawberries, blueberries, raspberries, kiwi, banana)
6 egg whites
1 1/2 cups sugar
1 1/2 teaspoons vinegar
1 teaspoon vanilla
1 pint whipping cream
Sugar to taste
Mint, fresh (for garnish)

Preheat oven to 300°F. Line cookie sheet with parchment paper. Beat egg whites until firm, add sugar gradually, and beat mixture until meringue is stiff and glossy. Add vanilla and vinegar.

Put mixture in a piping bag. Pipe a 4-inch round to form the bottom of the meringue, and then pipe a 1-inch side around the outside edge of each one. Bake the meringues for 1 hour, then turn off the oven and leave the meringues in to dry for another 1 hour.

Remove from oven and let cool (meringues can be saved in an airtight container for up to one week). To serve, whip cream and add sugar to taste. Place a meringue on a dessert plate, fill centre with whipped cream, and cover generously with fresh fruit and a sprig of mint.

Gowrie House
Sydney Mines

glen breton whisky, sticky lemon, and ginger cake

Makes 1 cake.

Whisky sauce

1 1/2 cups sugar
Juice of 1 fresh lemon
1/3 cups water
1/4 cup Glen Breton whisky

Combine all ingredients but the whisky in a small saucepan. Bring to a boil over medium heat. Boil mixture, stirring constantly, for 3 minutes. Remove from heat and let cool slightly. Stir in whisky.

Cake

2 cups butter
3 cups sugar
6 large eggs
1 cup crystallized ginger, finely chopped
1/3 cup ginger wine or syrup
Zest of 1 lemon
4 cups unbleached white flour
1/4 teaspoon salt
4 teaspoons Glen Breton whisky

Beat butter at medium speed with an electric mixer about 2 minutes or until soft and creamy. Gradually add sugar, beating at medium speed 5 to 7 minutes. Add eggs, one at a time, beating just until yellow disappears.

Add crystallized ginger, ginger syrup, lemon zest, and whisky. Combine flour and salt; add to butter mixture slowly, blending at low speed.

Pour batter into a greased and floured 10-inch tube or Bundt pan. Bake at 300°F for 1 hour and 40 minutes or until a wooden pick inserted in centre comes out clean. After 10 minutes cooling at room temperature, remove cake from pan and prick cake with long wooden pick at 1-inch intervals. Gradually pour whisky sauce over cake.

If desired, cake may be glazed while still warm with a mixture of 1 cup sifted icing sugar, 1 1/2 teaspoons of water or diluted lemon juice, and 1/2 teaspoon vanilla. Combine all ingredients, stirring well until smooth. Adjust consistency with more water or icing sugar, as required.

To serve, place slice of cake on a plate, drizzle with extra whisky sauce, and add a dollop of whipped cream. Garnish whipped cream with a mint leaf, if desired.

Allegro Grill and Deli
Sydney

chocolate caramel hazelnut tart

Makes one 4 x 10-inch tart.

Crust

1/2 teaspoon sugar
1 cup all-purpose flour
Pinch of salt
8 ounces unsalted butter, chilled and cut
  into 1/2-inch pieces
2 tablespoons cold water

Combine sugar, flour, and salt in mixer.
Cut in butter on low speed until pea-sized
pieces are formed. With mixer still on low
speed, add water and mix until dough just
comes together and is no longer dry. Shape
dough into a disc, cover in plastic wrap, and
refrigerate for 30 minutes.

Preheat oven to 350°F. Roll dough into
desired tart pan with a removable bottom.
Refrigerate shell for one hour, then bake for
25–30 minutes or until golden-brown.

Chocolate hazelnut filling

1 cup sugar
1/3 cup water
1 pint whipping cream (36%)
1 whole egg, slightly whipped
6 ounces hazelnuts, toasted and skinned
4 ounces bittersweet chocolate
2 tablespoons milk
1 ounce white chocolate

In a heavy-bottom saucepan, combine sugar
and water and dissolve over medium heat.

Increase heat and caramelize to amber
colour. Remove from heat and slowly add
cream (typically about one-quarter of total)
to desired thickness. Stir until smooth. Cool
slightly and add egg.

Put nuts in the bottom of the tart shell and
pour caramel mixture over nuts. Bake tart
for 20–25 minutes and let cool.

Melt chocolate with 1 tablespoon milk and
half of remaining cream. Repeat process
in a separate bowl with white chocolate
and remaining milk and cream. Spread
bittersweet chocolate and drizzle white
chocolate over top of tart and swirl.

Mescalero's
Sydney

restaurant guide

Allegro Grill and Deli in downtown Sydney is usually filled with happy diners and has developed some exciting and daring recipes.

L'Auberge Acadienne Inn on the Fleur-de-lis Trail in the village of Arichat features local seafood and Acadian specialties.

The Bankhead Pub in Inverness offers exquisite food in a casual and picturesque setting.

Bras d'Or Lakes Inn overlooks the St. Peter's canal and features some of the finest cuisine on the island.

The Cape Breton Smokehouse in Malagawatch near Marble Mountain is renowned for its smoked salmon and sausage.

The Cedar House in Seal Island is an extremely popular establishment. The parking lot is usually full and no one leaves hungry.

The Chanterelle Country Inn in North River, Victoria County, serves locally grown produce and features an adventurous menu.

The Cranberry Cove Inn on Wolfe Street in the historic seaport of Louisbourg features fresh seafood and comfortable surroundings.

Dundee Resort in Dundee, Richmond County, is set on a beautiful piece of property and a challenging golf course.

The English Country Garden Bed and Breakfast is located on a small lake in Indian Brook. Dinner here is an experience not to be missed.

Fourna Grill in the Ashby area of Sydney is a family-run Greek restaurant featuring the finest in Mediterranean cooking.

Gowrie House Country Inn in Sydney Mines combines elegant surroundings with top-notch dining.

The Grubstake Restaurant in Louisbourg has long been a local favourite for dinner after a trip to the fortress.

The Herring Choker Café is in Nyanza on the Trans-Canada Highway about fifteen minutes west of Baddeck. Homemade bread and baking highlight a delicious lunch menu.

Hôtel de la Marine at the Fortress of Louisbourg serves food the way it was prepared centuries earlier when the French fort was in operation.

Inverary Inn Resort in Baddeck is a resort that combines traditional and modern cuisine in a magnificent setting.

Island Sunset Resort in Belle Cote near Cheticamp is situated about as close to the Atlantic as possible. Spectacular views and delicious cuisine are to be expected.

Keltic Lodge Resort and Spa in Ingonish is an internationally respected establishment whose cuisine is both superb and exciting.

Lars Willum is the host and producer of the cable series *Be My Guest*. He also operates a catering business, Cape Breton Gourmet.

The Lobster Galley is just off the Trans-Canada Highway, twelve minutes from Baddeck, and has a lovely waterfront view. It can begin or end a drive around the Cabot Trail with splendid dining.

Main Street Café in Ingonish is at the gateway to the Cape Breton Highlands National Park and provides wonderful dining to complete a day of golfing or hiking.

The Markland Coastal Resort in Dingwall overlooks a pristine shoreline and offers comfort and elegance.

Mescalero's Open Grill Steak House in the Membertou Trade and Convention Centre in Sydney is a fashionable and innovative addition to local dining.

The Normaway Inn is nestled beautifully in the Margaree Valley. It is a long-time favourite renowned for salmon and lamb.

The Open Café in North Sydney specializes in vegetarian cooking and also offers organic fare.

Restaurant Acadien located in beautiful Cheticamp, Inverness County, specializes in home-cooked Acadian cuisine.

Riverbank Restaurant in Marion Bridge is a charming, family-run restaurant. It complements a lovely trip on the Mira.

The Water's Edge Inn, Café & Gallery in Baddeck is a fabulous location for lunch or a light dinner and is also a stunning gallery of Nova Scotian art.